The Geese Flew Over My Heart

Poems for Reflection and Prayer

— LYN MCCRAVE —

Sacristy
Press

Sacristy Press
PO Box 612, Durham, DH1 9HT

www.sacristy.co.uk

First published in 2019 by Sacristy Press, Durham

Sacristy Limited, registered in England & Wales, number 7565667

British Library Cataloguing-in-Publication Data
A catalogue record for the book is available from the British Library

ISBN 978-1-78959-017-3

For all who seek the mystery which is the God of Love

Preface

Over the last 50 years I have written poems reflecting my journey through life with God. I have selected 44 here and arranged them in six sections entitled *Awakening, Aspects of God, Finding God in Creation, Finding God in Ordinary Life, Sorrow and Joy* and *Prayers and Blessings.*

The first section, *Awakening*, is about the realisation of the desire within us for full union with God. There is a longing for self-giving, and a recipient inpouring from the mystery of God who is Love. We were created in God's image, and the seed of our desire to love and be loved was planted within us. As Augustine said in his *Confessions* "Our hearts are restless until they rest in You."

This awakening begins with a turning towards God, an invitation as expressed in the poem "Prayer of Openness", saying, however hesitantly, "Come". There is searching, loneliness and longing until finally we discover that what we are searching for is actually within us. Gradually a realisation dawns that we are utterly dependent on God, and peace comes with this acceptance. It is a love story like no other.

In this journey we experience different *aspects of God*. God is exquisitely gentle but then can appear to hide as in the poem "Evening". This is when our faith and trust is tested. But he is there within the darkness and never leaves us, as expressed in "Night Journeying", where we discover that the map through life is written in our hearts. We are little and vulnerable, but he is our Rock, the ground of our being. "God My Rock".

We find intimations of the presence of God in the beauty and mystery of *Creation*. It calls to us. We are at home here. In our place. We belong, and yet we move ever onwards.

But how can we ever fully know God unless he reveals himself in our humanity? This he has done perfectly in Christ, God made visible in a human being. He is the morning star pointing the way, showing us how to be fully human. We are called to follow. And his simple commandments are not based on dogma or church rules and regulations but on Love, for God and for our neighbour. It is not enough to have a personal relationship with God without expressing our love for God in our love and action for others and in our care for our unique selves.

So the fourth section is about *Finding God in Ordinary Life*. The God found in family life and work, in the frailty of ourselves and those we relate to. The God expressed in self- giving love and in compassion. The God we find by fully committing ourselves to others, where paradoxically we discover that self-giving leads to self-discovery and an enlarging of the heart. We become thus ever more authentically human.

In every life there is *sorrow and joy.* Inevitably, love leads to suffering and loss, for when we love, we suffer with the loved one's pain. We suffer at the state of our world. Suffering can lead to bitterness and turning from life, or it can lead to transformation, when our hearts become increasingly tenderised and vulnerable. Pierced and beautiful.

Mysteriously there can also be joy in sorrow, joy surviving and radiant despite sorrow. How can this be? It seems to me it is the light beyond this light, beauty beyond this world's beauty, breaking through, reminding us of resurrection, of our ultimate home and fulfilment.

The final section contains four simple prayers, but any of the poems may be used for reflection and prayer.

It is my hope that these poems may touch and comfort others, leading them to trust God, trust themselves, trust people and trust life. Love, suffer and pray. Be fully human and "All will be well and all manner of things will be well," as Julian of Norwich said in her *Revelations of Divine Love.*

A frail light flickers
Sprung from an eternal flame
Guard it; help it soar.

Contents

Awakening

Prayer of Openness

Here, God, I am.
Trembling.
Touch me.
Spirit of God,
O Love,
fill me.

Empty I am.
Broken.
Carved open deeply.
Painful.
Keen moist searing
Sorrowful longing.
Joy.
Love, spear me!
Spare me not.
I trust.

The Ascent

Lonely for love and a high mountain.
Heart of mine pierced and lost.
Taken away are my glens of rejoicing,
where mountain burns,
tumble into my longing,
cleansing me of all beseeching.

I need to pour out my strength for You
to be no more than empty
on a high crag,
awaiting Your descending,
so bending low for the summit
I climb.

Vigil

Dark, dark my heart,
and hard is this yearning.
My hearth is swept.
A fire for Your coming.

Down many roads have I walked.
You did not answer my calling.
Softly came the rain.
Night fell on my searching.

I thought to wander the moors,
with the wild birds crying.
The geese flew over my heart,
and I almost glimpsed You.

Is there a home for us,
a true belonging?
I wait for You.
A candle burns at my window.

Encounter

A meeting with the infinite

Before You I am
a quivering reed in the wind.
My form so simple.

Before You I extend
my open hands,
offering all my breathing.

Before You I bend low,
low as the sweet earth
from which I came.

Before You my heart whispers
that this
is the only Beauty.

Before You I know
the honours of others
are worthless.

Before You my tears
are a treasure
of reality.

Before You
I know myself,
and I am known.

Beneath the Mountain

Longing for union with God

In the shadow of the mountain,
I found my Love waiting.
He beckoned me,
and bade me come His way.

But I was full of trembling.
O, I was full of trembling.
Yet loving Him I could not turn away.

O my Love's face is beautiful,
and His gaze holds me,
and from Him I can never stay.

For He softly came towards me,
He gently came towards me,
and there beneath the mountain we did lay.

To the Beloved

Recognising utter dependence

Beloved, never leave me.

Though I am born of earth,

never leave me,

for all my heart's longings

are crowned in the Sun of Your Love.

And without you

I am the lonely wind

crying in the wilderness.

But come to me.

My lowly womb awaits Your Being

and the touch of Light.

O my Pure Love,

I am the dark earth

to be created as your lover.

Abandonment

Surrendering to God

I am Your little lover.
Come play with me.
I roam the hills
and lie in hidden places.

I have no worlds to conquer.
Come rest with me.
I was conquered long ago
and lie in Your arms vanquished.

See the sky bears no horizon,
and the geese skim the water,
and I sing to You
for no reason.

I am Your hidden lover,
and all worlds are here,
as You lie in my poverty,
and the wind ripples the water.

Winter

Listening in silence

Let me be still for one more winter
and nestle at my Love's feet.
The wild geese fly,
and my heart cries peace.

Let me lie with my Love
through the long dark nights,
with the north wind sighing.
Let me lie and listen to His whisperings.
When spring comes, I will fulfil them.

Aspects of God

Gentleness

My Beloved is gentle.
Gentle as a baby's sigh.
My beloved is
a cool balm
on my troubled brow.

Go gently.
Pause.
And watch
the raindrops
patterning the window.

The sea flows eternally.
An ebb and flow of mystery.
And we are one
in the silence
of being.

Evening

Be still and wait
in softly failing light.
The Beloved is at the gate
and sees me in love's night,
sitting in shadow.

Dear heart, do you not see
though all is dark and still.
You rest upon His knee.
So close is He, until
the dawn reveals Him.

Night Journeying

At night, as I unravel
like old frayed rope,
and the sea mist rolls
in over my horizon,
You are there.

I tremble and flow
this way and that
on the shifting tides.
Yet I know Your strong
hand rests on my tiller.

The rising waves slap hard
against my creaking bark,
as I hear you whisper
"Courage,
I have written the map on your heart."

God my Rock

I reached the pit
the end
the hard place.

Of no comfort
no energy
no life.

A barren land
stony
unforgiving
empty.

And staying there
holding on
dying
I whispered Your name.

And the rock became to me
my ground
my shelter
my comfort.

And the breath in me
Your breath
Your life
Your flowing.

Truly God is my rock
and my strength.

Finding God in Creation

Northumbria

By firelight,
by the waves' edge,
by the crying of the bird,
You heal me.

By silence,
by the sharing of the word,
by the roaring of the sea,
You heal me.

By the rock face,
by the ancient stones,
by the flowing of the past,
You heal me.

By laughter,
by a child's grace,
by the breaking of the bread,
You heal me.

Tigh an Rathaid

The house by the road

Between two burns, my Love has placed me.
Here by the curlew's haunts He bids me rest.
And all my wounds,
He bathes in beauty.

Tread softly here, tread softly.
The deer are roaming in the forest.
The robin slants his head,
and looks at me.

A mighty ocean is my Love,
and His waves have broken me.
Yet for His waters I thirst still,
and all my heart sings with His music.

Go gently here, go gently.
The tears of the mountains
are flowing in these burns.
My Love's and mine.

The love that wounded me will heal me.
And my joy will make Him whole.
By firelight we dance together,
a bridal dance.

Tread softly here, tread softly.
For the earth is touched by stars,
and beneath the frost
the snowdrops lie awake.

Highland Mornings

It is the mornings that I love,
the pink of the snow on the mountain,
the geese shouting for breakfast.

It is the morning air that greets me,
surprising me with freshness
and the breath of the silent pines.

It is the blue grey water flowing,
and the wise heron standing,
disregarding our haste.
It is the mornings that I love.

It is the sun rising on the hillside.
It is the mist dispersing.
It is the morning song in my broken heart.
It is the promise of life.
It is the promise of the Beloved's nearness.
It is the triumph of the Resurrection.

The Ploughed Field

Today, a ploughed field
stopped me as I walked.
Its rich, dark soil furrowed
deeply in my heart
and lifted me.

Why does this winter scene
move me so?
All green uprooted,
turned over.
All aglow with waiting.

This emptiness is full of life.
The energy of seasons past
flows within,
as silently it rests.
A hushed expectancy
of new sowing.

Hebridean Retreat

Fill me up, Lord.
My well is empty.
I thirst for flowing waters
and the sound of the sighing wind.

Fill me with waves crashing
onto empty beaches,
with wide skies and
rain drifting gently on hills.

May the ravens' call and
the cry of lapwings lift me,
as the emerging sun sparkles
on my grey spirit, like
light illuminating the lochans.

Seals rest where otters play,
and the deepening silence
echoes within, drawing
me to stillness.

A sacred Presence breathes
through all things.

And joy sings in Creation.

Finding God in Life

Ubi Christus est?

And all the while I'm writing
and am learning,
let me be
deepening in knowledge
of Christ in unity
with all the world.

And all the days I'm speaking
and am laughing
with the crowd.
Love within,
may I find You
whom we shroud.

Meeting

I will remember today.
For the moment your gaze
met mine,
I saw your heart's gentleness
flowing in your eyes.

I will remember your smile.
And those unspoken tears,
which lingered there a while
and sang to me.

Which Way?

A young doctor's discernment

I walk alone.
The desert is dry and barren.
I am told that this is a vale of loveliness.

My tongue is parched.
I ask for rivers.
People flow past unendingly.

Oh my body is cold,
I tremble for warmth
"Wait till summer," they say.

But the blind-eyed people who speak
are trembling too
and speeding past with dry lips.

I look in the eyes of the sick.
The world's sorrow beckons me,
and I enter at a glance.

The white-coated people
speak of the tests
but touch not our being.

And I stand by the bed
in a white coat
and weep alone.

I have walked near flowing waters
and felt the touch of Love.
The only healing.

And I can remember when
I saw my Beloved smiling
behind the pleading eyes of pain.

So shall I rise,
casting off this iron coat,
and seek the Healer in the wilderness.

To a Boy Born with a Withered Arm

Child with the withered arm,
new-born man a-growing,
slowly you wake.
And I who watch and bless you
know in my heart
that pain awaiting
all your awakening.

Where will your manhood lie,
O little warrior?
Where is your strength?
Not for you the mountains
or the snow-capped pinnacles.
But in some lonely valley,
by hidden streams,
the frail world will deliver up its mystery.

Extreme Premature Triplets

I watched a mother stand alone,
beholding her sons.
All three of them
stretched out
in an agony of breathing.

And I felt her tears in my heart
keenly,
though none will know the depth of them,
except, perhaps, that other Mother.

Was it for this they were born,
that sweet flesh should lose its warmth
in the shock of suffering?

Her eyes searched me,
and I, remembering Mary,
touched her arm
and was silent.

The Tree on Waste Ground

I can take you to a place
in this grey city,
where a tree wearies itself
growing in the desolation.
And you will find joy at the sight of it,
for it is the continuing Redemption.

So too, my Love, you and I
weary ourselves with giving.
We lose our lives in loving.
We ache and bleed,
and so find Life.
Here in this city.
Like battered trees we smile at the tenements.

For My Father in Old Age

Gasping for breath I found him
there on the top stair of his life.
Frail bones bending.
And I remembered him strong and lending
all his strength for others.
Speech was choked from him.
Nothing but breathing left,
and a painful sighing.
Pain in my heart too,
and I was crying with him.

Then his rare blue eyes met mine,
betraying his fear.
But I loved him more then
than in the high days of his manhood,
when a little girl sang from his shoulder.

On Crossing the Border

For my Mother with Alzheimer's

There are other countries,
other lands to meet,
more lovely than the wave-lapped shore.

There are other places
than the ones we knew,
other woods to wander in our gathering.

There are other songs
than the shared times of evening
and the music of a thousand days.

Little Mother.

There is another home
than the homes we shared,
even deeper than belonging.

Where time and memory have ceased,
and nothing is lost
in the Kingdom of the Heart.

Little Mother.

A Parent's Farewell

I always seem to be saying goodbye,
packing your boat,
launching you out

into the deep.

Then I stand and wait for your wave,
that smile that says
"Here I go; stay there.
Be my harbour."

February Morning in Retirement

The geese are finding their voices.
Broken cackles
on dark mornings.
A restlessness for the North.
And hidden shoots
unfurl in freedom.
Called into being
by a whisper of warmth.
The long night closes,
as a faint light
streaks the dawn.
And my broken voice
sings once more.

Haiku for an Unborn Grandchild

Your lips are forming,
as she knits for you a prayer.
A call to being.

Sorrow and Joy

Miscarriage

Little being,
touching my womb with life,
our lives with wonder.
Why did you leave so soon?
Was there no room
within us
for your growing?

Little being,
the first fruit of our love
and all our giving.
We rounded you with care
and silent prayer
for all your living.

Little babe,
but fleetingly you stayed
within my womb
at snowdrop time
like other loves
you left too soon.

Cradle Song

After a second miscarriage

Be at peace, my little ones.
And may the Mother of all,
the Mother of Himself,
be watching your growing.
As surely as she watches us,
guiding our faltering hearts
to the hidden truth
in pain and blood flowing.
We have lost your lovely limbs,
the sight of your flowering.
And no-one now need rock your cradle.

But the life you left in your dying
grows in our brokenness,
as we rock each other.

Snowdrops

Snowdrops
bursting through winter
with infinite weakness
stronger than hard earth
miraculous growing
are showing now
growing
making my hope alive.

O bless me
broken and bleeding
who have laid My Love to rest
dear flesh
into the dark earth
that is all taking
breaking
awakening
to snowdrops.

Unless a grain of wheat . . .

Dreams in daytime weariness
are menacing my heart,
enmeshing me in memory,
tearing me apart,
insisting that I listen,
and let the grieving start.

Come and let the rains fall,
softening up the earth.
Come and let the frost bring
truth to a new birth.
Come and let the healing
heal and bring new mirth.

So the Voice is whispering.
Peace is born of pain.
So the Presence teaches me.
Nothing dies in vain.
Tears are for the sowing.
Bread of Life from grain.

A Solway Evening

Strong are the Solway tides
and strong my grief.
My heart's anguish rides
wild as the wild geese
over the sunlit sands
to the sinking sun.
Then I stand alone
in the empty Solway night,
waiting for a star to rise.
and my heart's tenderness
like a dying sun
floods the Earth.

A Hidden Grieving

*After hearing of a mother who kept her expressed
breast milk frozen after her baby's death*

For ten years she kept it
hidden
after he died.

Her very essence,
squeezed out
drop by drop.

All her tenderness
and nurturing
frozen in time

like her dreams
and the seed
of his flowering.

A link too sacred
to be discarded
without ceremony.

Milk for her baby.

Joy and Sorrow

Joy will come in the evening.

Quietly.

Like rays of light

sifting softly through clouds,

she will find the hidden lake

of all my sorrow.

And blessing me,

caressing low as the swallows,

my darkened being will shine.

A thousand caverns.

A thousand mysteries

of love and bleeding.

And the lake's depths will equal the mountains.

For a Loved One in Tears

I would spare you all tears,
round you with my love:
a protective shield.

And yet, your tears are precious.
They touch my heart,
and I know your beauty.

Your littleness echoes mine,
calling us to greatness.

Tears of Gratitude

So, here you are,
surprising me. Your honesty
opening my heart
like peeled fruit.
For beauty has pierced
me through to thankfulness,
illuminating all memory.
For this is true: though sorrow
is real, love is stronger.
And love is all.

Yellowhammers

For a terminally ill friend

I promise you yellowhammers
on a Spring day.
I will wrap you up
warm against the chill.
And wheel you up
that lane you love.
And when you see that golden wave
rising from the hedgerows,
we'll stop. And smile.
Time will cease in that moment.
And all pain.
There will just be light
glinting on wing tips.
And birdsong.

Ageing

When your bones tell you
that winter approaches,
and you sit more than
you walk,
there is still time.

When inspiration leaves you,
and the day seems long
and grey,
there is still growth.

When you are forced
into stillness,
though your heart is
climbing mountains,
there is great gift.

For when you say yes,
deep within your littleness,
the Spirit is creating
miracles.

Prayers and Blessings

Dressing Prayer to the Trinity

As I clothe myself this morning, o God,
preparing to meet the Great Elements,
may I be clothing myself
in the Light and Strength of the Father.

May I be clothing myself
in the Peace and Joy of the Son.

May I be clothing myself
in the Love and Wisdom of the Spirit.

With Mary around and Michael guarding.
With Mary around and Michael guarding.

Amen.

Prayer on the Road

O Thou Great God,
grant us each day
something of the morning freshness,
the sun lifting the dew.

O Thou Creator of All,
grant us the wisdom
to give ourselves
a little resting.

For the song in us
is our bread
and the dance
part of our journeying.

O Thou Great God,
grant us each day
a stopping place by the waters.

Blessing for a Marriage

May you walk the tide line,
that sacred space,
where frailty meets grace
and wonder.

May you create
in gentleness
a dance of being,
opening to life.

May you go forth boldly,
with Christ, your light,
the guiding star
of all humanity.

And may the God
of all things
fill your hearts,
and make them one.

Amen.

Night Blessing for a Loved One

God cradle you in tenderness, my love,
and watch you sleep and guide you through the stars.
All night long may rivers from you flow
and bathe the earth.

God speak to you in silence, o my love,
and fill your heart to make it as His own.

With every beat the pulse of life is thrown
along your veins.

Acknowledgements

The poem "Joy and Sorrow" was previously published in *Presence: An International Journal of Spiritual Direction* in March 2015. I would like to thank my commissioning editor Natalie Watson for her patience in guiding this book to fruition.

I thank Sister Eileen Cassidy of the Ignatian Spirituality Centre, Glasgow, Sister Angela of Pauline Books and Media, Glasgow, and the Kelvingrove Writers Group, of which I am a member, for their encouragement. I also thank my friend Margie Weir Cairns, who gave up her time reading through my poems. I greatly appreciated her wisdom and advice. Also Muriel Wilson, who listened often and supported always. And finally my husband, who gives me the space I need to write and on whose love I lean.